Essence of Black Love

The Blueprint

Written By: Bobbie Michelle Bean & Donny Young

Library of Congress: Catalogue-in-Publication Data, available upon request

ISBN: 9798708600301

Printed in the USA

Bobbie Bean Publishing LTD

www.bobbiebean.com

Editor: Brandi Jefferson

Cover Photo: Karen Marie Images

Graphic Design: Nate Ward KN8 Design

Synopsis

Essence of Black Love: The Blueprint is an exploration of black love through African American music, culture, history, and through the Word of God. This manual examines the intricacies associated with our blackness and consequently our relationships and offers wisdom and guidance with which to manage them.

Fall in love with love as you develop a deeper, more insightful understanding of your mate and yourself. Learn strategies and best practices that enhance your relationship with each implementation, leading you closer and closer to a forever kind of love.

Comedic interludes, sincere discovery, and genuine solutions not only make *Essence of Black Love: The Blueprint* an incredible read, but it puts *forever* well within reach. You will laugh, you will cry, and you will learn the reasons why. *Essence of Black Love: The Blueprint* is an investment in your relationship intended to bring you and the one you love years of happiness.

Essence of Black Love: The Blueprint is a waltz between male and female, offering perspectives from both sides of the same coin. Set in present-day, this manual provides real applications for exponential growth in your relationship in the life and times in which we currently live. *Essence of Black Love: The Blueprint* establishes basic principles to love by and offers strategies that cultivate a healthy, happy, sustainable, long-lasting black love relationship.

Table of Contents

Chapter 1: Tell Me

Female Perspective

Tell me what you want. Tell me what you need. Tell me if it ain't good enough for you, babe. Tell me…

Sis, if you are not telling your mate what you want and need, how will he know to give it to you? I hear women say time and time again, "I will never ask a man for anything." Well, sis, if this is you, don't ever expect to get what you want from any man. I haven't seen a man with a crystal ball yet.

Mama taught me, "Closed mouths don't get fed." We adhere to this wisdom at work. We adhere to this in restaurants. We adhere to this at the beauty shop, the spa, the department store… Why, then, do we not adhere to this when it comes to our relationships? What makes us choose to close our mouths rather than eat?

Are we afraid what we say will fall on deaf ears? Do we feel if we ask for what we need, we might be seen as "needy?" Are we afraid he will leave if we require more effort, more time, more energy, etc.?

If the answer to any of these questions is yes, why are you with that person?

I don't know about you, but I am not prepared to be in a relationship where my needs are not being met for five minutes. Let alone a lifetime. And I am certainly not ready to put my time and energy into something that would not yield the return I'm seeking because time and energy are the most valuable assets I or anyone else can give.

By no means am I suggesting that you quit your relationship because you "think" the answers would be yes. What I am suggesting you do is have the conversation.

Talk to your mate. Open your mouth and give him an opportunity to prove you wrong. Tell your man," I'm hungry." Give him a chance to feed you.

All too often, women will suffer in silence, get angry in silence, get frustrated in silence, grow bitter in silence, and then blame the man for not loving us right. However, what we must do instead is ask ourselves, "Did we allow him to?"

We are so worried about being INDEPENDENT and able to do for ourselves. We are so concerned with proving we don't need a man for anything that we starve ourselves to death, or in other words, we break up. NOT FAIR!

If you have not told your man the desires of your heart, you did not give him or your relationship a chance. The only man that knows the desires of your heart without you telling him is God. So, before you call it quits, take the advice of Dru Hill, and tell him what you want. Tell him what you need. Tell him if it ain't good enough for you, babe. Tell him.

Furthermore, don't stop telling him, because the twenty-year-old you does not want the same thing the thirty-year-old you want. The thirty-year-old you does not want the same things fifty-year-old you want. So, as your needs change, so should your conversation.

Male Perspective

Tell him what you want. Tell him what you need. Tell him if it ain't good enough for you, babe. Tell him…

All too often, I hear men say. "I don't know what this woman wants from me." My immediate response is, "Did you ask her?" When the answer is yes, my follow up question is, "Did you listen?" If that answer is yes, I ask. "What behaviors did you modify, and what action did you take to prove that?"

If the first two questions did not stump them, unfortunately, the third usually does.

The Bible deems the man head of household, instructed to cover, protect and provide. Consequently, a man often exudes that dominant nature in their relationship.

The word dominate means to have a commanding influence on or exercise control over. To simplify, a man will naturally do more directing and insisting than asking and listening. So, while we may not control our mate with words, we will control our mate with actions; and since dominance is in our nature, the actions by which we control our spouse are not always intentional or conscious efforts — subconscious kicks in where nature is involved. Now, with natural instinct forever at work, we have to make a conscious and deliberate effort to counter that.

Before we assume that we know what our women want, we need to ask, or at the very least, confirm what we are giving our woman is what she actually wants.

Dr. Stephen Covey in *7 Habits of an Effective Leader* says that most people do not listen with the intent to understand. They listen to reply. Therefore, I challenge you, men, to be mindful. Ask yourself, are you listening for understanding or to reply? Make sure that you make a habit of listening to understand. For only through understanding are we able to make the changes our women need.

Understanding allows you to do more than just react, respond, or adjust for the moment. Understanding allows you to know when to apply requested actions without being asked to do so each time. Understanding allows for anticipation and proaction. If I have a complete understanding of what my wife needs, wants, and expects, whether in church or out on the town, I know what triggers her and can avoid pulling that trigger.

On the contrary, when listening is not used for understanding, we are destined to be repeat offenders. So when she is trying to tell you what she wants, don't just listen — understand!

How does one gain understanding? Ask open-ended questions, then be quiet. Tell me more about that... How did you feel when? What was it about my actions that bothered you? What do you need me to do differently? What should I have done differently? How can I prevent this from happening moving forward? Ask questions until you overstand. Once you believe you have it, repeat it back and then ask if your understanding is correct. Finally, ask if she would like to add and or deduct anything from what you've repeated back to her.

Now for the good part, the stumper... modify your behavior and your actions to accomplish the change your mate is seeking. Accommodate her needs within reason. For example, if more time is needed, map out a date day. Each of you can take turns planning. Make a game out of it. See who can come up with the best date night. Place a fun wager on it. Perhaps you're on a budget. See who can come up with the best date for less than $20. Maybe you need some spice. Create new firsts with your mate. Think outside the box. Make a date of rock climbing or ax throwing, maybe couples' karate. Whatever it is, as long as you are together, seek out new firsts.

It's essential to remember to make a habit of this behavior and action modification. Be consistent with the new behaviors and actions to the point they become second nature. This is the point at which your woman will know she is heard.

Chapter 2: Head of Household

What dictates the Head of Household, and why does that matter? Let's take a look.

The Bible states in I Corinthians 11:3, *"But I would have you know that the head of every man is Christ, and the head of the woman the man...*

The IRS deems the head of household as the taxpayer, who pays more than half the cost of keeping up a home for the tax year.

By familial standards, the head of household is that person who has the final say.

So, which is right? Who then is the head of household when a black man and black woman beat the tremendous odds stacked against them to become one? Will it be determined by gender, by money, or by power?

Female Perspective

Traditionally speaking, the "Head of Household" was the man by God's design. The man's responsibility was to provide for his wife and children and make decisions on behalf of his family. This is what made a man a man. The woman's job was to care for the children and be submissive to her husband. She was to be a lady, seen and not heard. Fast forward to 2020, and we are light-years away from this notion.

For over 100 years, women have fought for equal rights, equal pay, and equal status, but black women in America have fought this fight for centuries. In Sojourner Truth's *Ain't I A Woman*, she says,

> *Look at me, look at my arms, I have plowed, and planted, and gathered in the barns, and no man can head me. And ain't I a woman? I could work as much and eat as much as a man when I could get it and bear the lash as well. And ain't I a woman? I have borne 13 children and seen most all sold off to slavery. And when I cried out with my mother's grief no one but Jesus heard me. And ain't I a woman?*

I reference this speech not only for its accuracy but to illustrate a critical point. Sofia, in *The Color Purple*, was not at all lying when she said, *"All my life, I had to fight."*

The black woman in America has had to fight her entire life, and she has had to do so alone. Because of the systematic and deliberate destruction of the black family in America, courtesy of slavery and the injustice system amongst other things, the black woman was taught something no other culture teaches their women — I-N-D-E-P-E-N-D-E-N-C-E.

The black woman was forced to stand alone in the fields as her husbands and sons were sold off, while women in other cultures were encouraged to marry and build families. The black woman was taught to wear the pants in her household working the jobs denied our men, while women in other cultures were taught that they look good in skirts. Black women were left to be the pillars in our families, fending for and tending to their children alone, while women in other cultures were taught that burden falls on the man's shoulders. Rather than consider these social constructs in an attempt to better understand the black woman, society labels us.

Angry, aggressive, difficult, controlling, and overbearing are frequently used to describe the black woman, which is painful enough. To add insult to injury is the fact that all too often, these negative descriptions come from the lips of our black men. That being said, it is crucial to understand how this conundrum manifests itself in relationships, making it difficult to come together, defining roles, and particularly determining who is the head of household.

Male Perspective

Black men in America have never been viewed as equal. As slaves, we were forced to take the slave *master's* name, stripping us of our identity. We were bred like animals. We were forced to watch our women and children tortured before being sold off to the next plantation, separating us from our family and rendering us powerless.

A black man could not look a white man in the eye, stripping us of our pride. We were to be subservient and to step and fetch. Even after "emancipation," black men were denied any job opportunities that would allow us to support our families, making necessary the financial contribution of our women in direct violation of our kingly nature.

Fast forward to 2020, not much has changed. Black men are still public enemy number one in a society that makes every attempt to beat us down. To this day, every institution in this country is designed to set us up for failure. Despite the tremendous strides we have made, we continue to be plagued by a slave mentality those years of mental and emotional tyrannies have etched in our DNA. We wrestle against principalities such as the need to exert authority, absenteeism in the household, and a disdain for ourselves and, by default, our ribs, also known as our black women.

So, here we have two sides to the same coin. On the one side, you have a woman who yearns for protection, support and love, a shoulder on which to lean. Yet, she does not know how to accept it as she has been taught to be superwoman, made of steel, unbreakable, unyielding, and conditioned to travel through life alone.

On the other side of that coin, you have a man searching to find his rightful place in a world that has rendered him powerless. You have a man wanting nothing more than to carve out space where he can be king of his castle.

Quite evident is how these two can bump heads. So how, instead, do we merge these two conflicted individuals into one?

Male Perspective

To love the black woman, the black man more than anyone should understand that the label society places on her should not be hated but respected, admired, and appreciated. Rather than break, as America would have her, the black woman evolved. She showed strength where people wanted her to show weakness. She showed fearlessness when people wanted her to be afraid. She showed courage when people wanted her to concede. Those negative adjectives used to describe our women are the very slurs spewed at her when she is on the frontline fighting for us, shoulder to shoulder, fighting with us and by herself fighting in spite of us. At no point in history has our black woman been saved by the bell, free to drop her guard, put her fists down, and take a breath.

We should let no one despise and attempt to shame our black women for their strength, a strength that continues to amaze and bewilder. Now more than ever, we must take the time to understand our women and what it has taken and continues to take to survive as a black woman in America, a plight that is a direct parallel to ours. Rather than aid and abet our women's crucifixion, we as black men must learn to protect our women, communicate with our women, have patience with our women and nurture our women. We must evolve into the men that our women can trust enough to drop her fists and finally rest.

Female Perspective

To love the black man, the black woman more than anyone should understand the depths to which his manhood and very essence have been attacked. America has had its foot on the neck, a noose on the neck, barbed wire on the neck, a chokehold on the neck of the black man since he arrived in this land. Every institution has told him he is nothing in an effort to usurp his authority in all capacities. The last thing we as black women should do is aid in his destruction. Yet, we do just that. We aid in his demise with the words that we speak. Every time we say to our black man, "We don't need you for anything..." Every time we curse our black men, calling them out of their names, berating them with their shortcomings, in public, in private, in front of the kids, we are willingly participating in the emasculation of our fathers, sons, husbands, and brothers.

Life and death are in the power of the tongue. We must breathe life into our men and create that space for them to be restored to their rightful place. Contrary to what the world would have the black woman believe, we were not designed to journey through life alone. We are queens deserving of our kings, but WE have to crown them.

Ok, we've peeled back some layers and established some framework to better manage one another. Now, let's continue with the task at hand, which is deciding what dictates the head of household and why this is paramount to a relationship's success.

Female Perspective

When researching this subject, nowhere does it state that all black women subscribe to traditional roles, nor do we have to, and nowhere does it state all black men do, either. That is totally fine. However, no one should move forward with a serious relationship without first establishing a clear understanding of your mate's expectations concerning this matter. Even more critical is being certain where you truly stand on the issue. That certainty begins with an understanding and consideration of one's nature when thinking long term.

See, anyone can function in an unnatural state temporarily. Still, if that is truly not your design, you will not be able to function in that position for an extended period of time. Consider this simple analogy. Ladies, this will probably resonate with you the most.

You walk into a store and fall in love with the perfect shoe for an outfit you're dying to wear. You ask the clerk for your size. They check the back. Your size is not there. They check the system. The shoe is sold out except for the one pair which is in your hand and happens to be a size too small. Ladies, what happens next?

We buy the shoe and purpose in our hearts and minds to wear the shoe long enough to walk into the event looking extra fly. Maybe we can muster out a two-step and a photo or two, but at some point, we know the nerve endings in our feet will reject the tight space we've stuffed them into and will send messages to our brain in the form of excruciating pain. *"Warning! Warning! Time to vacate!"* At that point we can either remove the shoes or suffer the long-term consequences, which are quite unpleasant.

Think about this. Whether considering a professional role or a personal role, the shoe scenario holds true. Have you ever heard the saying *fake it 'til you make it?* Business owners pay thousands of dollars per employee to administer assessment tests that reveal a person's true nature for this very reason. They know people will fake it 'til they make it and, when tired of faking it, will exit stage left. So, to thwart high turnover rates, employers administer these tests to make sure they are hiring people for their right fit roles in the first place. This saves an employer time, resources, and money, six months down the line when the employee can no longer pretend. If employers consider a person's natural disposition when filling a role, why wouldn't we consider our natural disposition when accepting a role?

Too often, we become strangers in our houses because we faked the funk long enough to lock down someone by playing a role that we are not prepared to play for the next two years. Forget about the rest of our lives! So, how do we avoid this? We avoid this by first being honest with ourselves. Then once we have a clear understanding of self, we have to understand the other party.

The black woman has had to become the most educated human on the planet in an effort to debunk a system that still sees her as less than. Consequently, the black woman often puts herself in a position to hold a higher status than her black male counterpart. Sixty-five percent of working black women hold white-collar jobs compared to 42% of black men (*blackdemographics.com,* 10/19).

When considering black women make up 53% of the black labor force, that disparity increases. More often than not, the black woman is the primary breadwinner and, by IRS standards, head of the house. Furthermore, in 2018 there were 4.04 million households run by a single black mother (*Statista.com* 11/19). While this does not mean the father was absent from the child's life, it means he was absent from the child's home. That being said, the final word in that household was the woman's. So, by familial standards, the black woman wins again. Even so, is this really what we want?

Women, are we happy being the head of household, or are we just good at it out of necessity? Do we want a man to lighten our load or flat out tell us, "Sit down, I got this!"?

This is such a critical discovery because if we truly do not want to be head of household yet settle for someone who makes less than us, or who cannot take the lead and elevate us, eventually we will resent that person.

On the same note, if we are career-driven women, caring less about who makes the most money and more about support with our kids and support with household responsibilities, we should be looking for that man who can offer that type of support. Settling for someone who just wants us to quit our jobs or who cannot value our goals will ultimately lead to that same resentment.

Male Perspective

Men, do we even need a woman who wants to submit to her man? Would we have issues with our woman making more than us like Martin did Gina? Each of these questions must be explored because a woman could be the primary breadwinner and still want to submit, for whatever reason. In that case, could we learn to be ok with that, or would we continuously find ways to tear our woman down in other areas as punishment for her success?

What if our black woman doesn't want to submit, regardless? Would we be in a constant state of competition because of our own insecurities, or could we break those mental chains slavery endowed us with and be confident and secure in our manhood, regardless?

Maybe we don't care for the title head of household. Perhaps we need a woman who wants the title and goes half-sies on everything, so we don't bear the burden alone. Are we ok doing household chores and having a meal on the table because our woman is a hard-working career woman?

Paramount to any relationship's success is knowing and understanding where both parties stand, not at the end but at the beginning of the relationship. Notice I said relationship, not situationship, not entanglement, but relationship!

Mind you. If you're dealing with a person who is merely temporary and nothing long-term, then no need for a deep dive.

Conversely, the minute that changes, put your suit on, grab your goggles and go swimming. Failing to do so will result in one or both parties feeling unfulfilled and unsatisfied because it is just not what they really want.

Moreover, if you ignore your true nature long enough to have kids involved and families vested, everybody suffers over something that could have been avoided from the jump, just by being honest and transparent. So, do not do it. Take time to figure this out before going too deep. Do the legwork.

Establish who has the final say when a disagreement occurs? Do we have an equal say and decide with rock, paper scissors? Do one of the two parties concede his or her vote, not wanting that responsibility? Does one's opinion rank higher than the other? Do we draw straws? Is it situational based on your area of expertise? For example, does the man have the final say on the parental strategies and the wife the final word on financial strategies?

Asking questions such as these and establishing Head of Household is a very necessary step in determining long term compatibility capabilities which are very necessary to ensure we are in alignment and on our right path with our right fit person.

Chap 3: Equally Yoked

Female Perspective

What does it mean to be equally yoked, and why is this so important?

To understand what equally yoked means, we must first understand what a yoke is.

Oxford Languages defines a yoke as "a wooden crosspiece that is fastened over the necks of two animals and to the plow or cart they are to pull." Therefore, to be yoked is to be tethered to someone for the sake of pulling together.

So what does equally yoked mean?

For years, I heard pastors, preachers, deacons, and church mothers regurgitate the same verse over and over, *Be ye not unequally yoked together with unbelievers* (II Cor 6:14). Consequently, I grew up believing to be unequally yoked meant nothing more than I, as a Christian, could not become one with a Muslim or Jehovah's Witness or Buddhist or any faith other than Christian. Who knew there was more to the story?

Although I had never heard by way of a sermon, I discovered the Bible, in Deuteronomy, warns us against plowing with an ox and an ass together. Having no extensive knowledge about either of the two beasts, easy was determining why this was not a good idea, and even easier was determining how this expounds upon the notion of being unequally yoked.

The ox is much bigger and stronger than the ass, thus making a synchronized pull impossible. After further exploration of the subject, I found that an oxen's temperament allows for effective training and obedience to a master. Whereas the donkey is stubborn and unwilling to cooperate, further compromising the pull as the donkey struggles to detach from the ox to go his separate way. These factors alone make each animal a detriment to the other if yoked together.

While the Bible is an efficient instrument, and this was useful, practical advice, I doubt very seriously Moses was merely talking about animals. The animals were used to illustrate something so many of us fail to realize until we are tethered to an ass in a relationship that is destined to fail.

When choosing a mate, one must consider the other's size and strength. Now, I'm not talking size and strength in the literal sense, but more so in the figurative sense. In other words, I'm talking load bearing calculation. How big are your mate's shoulders, and how much weight can he or she bear without breaking? How much weight do they want to carry? Let me explain.

I have never lacked ambition. I strived to be the best. Yet, in my younger years, my requirement for a man did not take into consideration ambition. I wanted brown skin, a bangin' body, and attention. So, the family joke becoming, "Who's coming to Thanksgiving dinner this year?" should not have come as a surprise.

My list of requirements was too short. I needed to add a thing, or two, or three. I needed to require of my mate what I require of myself. If I was going to have a long-term relationship, my mate's ambition had to match mine, and so should yours.

Maybe you don't want the white picket fence, 2.5 kids, and a dog. Perhaps you just want a light load that consists of a job, not a career, and endless free falling. That is your prerogative. Just make sure your mate has the same desire, or lack thereof. On the flip side, if you are ready to take over the world, you need an ox prepared to do the same, ready to pull that heavy load. Upon having this epiphany, I did just that.

I met a man with beautiful brown skin, a nice body, and a drive that matched mine. I fell head over heels in love. Oh, it was on and popping. We got married. I had his child, and then we were separated, and not by choice. My daughter grew up without a father in the home because he spent the rest of her childhood in prison.

I had forgotten the other part of the equal yoke equation. Sure, my pick was built to sustain a heavy load like me, but he was stubborn and not at all interested in journeying down the same path. I learned the hard way we were not headed in the same direction, so we could not pull together.

See, although we started at the same point, the further we journeyed down those separate paths, the further apart we drifted. Quickly, the load shifted completely, and I ended up pulling alone. When I got tired of bearing the load and the deadweight added due to poor choices, we decided to end the marriage.

Now, since I understand *Reason, Season, Lifetime,* I have no regrets. He and I came together for a reason — my daughter — the best thing that ever happened to me. We were together for a season, a season that allowed me to truly understand what Moses meant when he said don't plow with an ox and donkey together. This experience grew me to the point of understanding what I want and need to sustain a lifetime.

Male Perspective

So, what does equally yoked mean?

For years I grew up hearing, *"You can't turn a hoe into a housewife."* Not 'til my adult years did I develop an adult understanding of what this meant. I was digesting this statement in a very black and white, literal sense, not considering the levels to it.

Since I would never use the term hoe when referencing any woman and certainly not my queen, we are going to use the name Holly in lieu of hoe for the sake of this illustration.

Between Holly and housewife are a lot of women. There's the girlfriend, the independent woman, the baby mama, the kept wife, the career wife, the soccer mom, and so much more. Just like you can't turn a Holly into a housewife, you can't turn a housewife into a Holly. The problem for many of us is that we do not take the time to find out which woman we want before tethering to the woman we are with.

Marriage is not the only way a person becomes tethered to someone. A baby tethers two people together for at least eighteen years. Major purchases and living arrangements tether. Sex tethers. Commitment tethers. So before committing to any of these acts, one may want to consider why the warning was issued.

Similar to the Bible's warning against the yoking of an ox and an ass, the Holly to housewife warning was issued to illustrate much the same. The reality is you cannot make someone become who they are not. So, recognize them for who they are, be it an ox or an ass or whatever lies between them and deal accordingly.

In my early twenties, I was only concerned with having fun. I was not trying to wife anyone up. So, I primarily dealt with women who felt the same way. They weren't in it for anything serious. We were just friends with benefits, or at least I thought so. The problem was that I loved all types of women. I was attracted to housewives, for example, and although they professed with their mouths that they wanted nothing serious, their behaviors indicated otherwise. Rather than accept them for who they showed me they were, I focused on what I wanted. I was having fun, and although I knew better, I allowed them to catch feelings and eventually expect something I was not prepared to give them. Men, this is always a prelude to a stalker type situation, a paternity test, a woman scorned, etc., and trust when I say does more harm than good. I ruined friendships and lost acquaintances.

As I grew older and started looking for something more meaningful, I looked for that lady in the streets and a freak in the sheets. I believed I could proceed in much the same manner I had already functioned. I believed I could date a woman under the auspices we would date, get to know each other, and not place titles on what we had, thinking that when I decided I wanted something more, she would follow suit. That didn't work either. I quickly learned how the housewives felt that I tried to turn into Hollies.

I concluded that before I start "dating" a woman, I would do a better job of sizing her up first, determining her load calculations.

Now, I had come to know a young lady who was sexy like I like. Like she wore suits to work to mask what she was working with. If you didn't know, black women are tried for having curves in the corporate world. I digress. We'll get to that later.

Like I was saying, she was sexy and wore suits to work to tone down all she'd been blessed with. She loved to kick it and have fun, but never at the expense of her career. She worked at the hospital and was passionate about her work. I could see she was a nurturer. She carried herself in a manner where she was accessible but nowhere near easy, and this to me was an indication I might be on the right path.

I proceeded with caution and adopted practices that were conducive to building real relationships. Out of those practices I adopted, the most important was communication. Rather than assume I knew this woman and her wants and desires, I asked her. I asked her what she wanted out of life. I paid attention to verbal and nonverbal cues. I got to know her family to see what she was accustomed to.

It turns out I was right about this one. I found my ox to be tethered to. I identified my sweet spot between Holly and housewife and found her, that person with whom I could be equally yoked. She wanted the same things out of life that I wanted. She wanted a mate to grow and build with and create a legacy, and she did not want to do that prematurely, so we took our time.

We worshiped the same God, shared the same beliefs, one of which was family first. So, when we got married and had our child, the pull became easier, not harder. We were in sync as we continued our pull toward greatness together.

Now, I would be remiss if I didn't mention another component to being equally yoked, and this too stems from something that I heard growing up that took on a whole new meaning as an adult. For years, I heard, *"If she can't use your comb, don't bring her home."* As a child, I believed this to be more about lice than life. However, as a black man in America, I understand this to be so much greater.

While we would love to believe we being of the human race, are all the same… you know we bleed the same blood and all, there is a huge difference in one of the major systems that make up a human's anatomy, and that is the integumentary system. The integumentary system consists of hair, skin, and nails, and the primary function of this system is to act as a barrier, protecting the body from the outside world. Furthermore, the integumentary system is the only system visible to the naked eye; and although meant to protect the body from the outside world, for black people, this is not the case.

That same barrier that is protection for whites is a bullseye for blacks. Black people in America are persecuted for the melanin in their integumentary systems. This, in turn, creates an experience that is unique to people of color. It is an experience that cannot be denied as much as people would like to. It creates an experience that makes us susceptible to unfair and unjust treatment. It creates an experience that shapes who we are and adds a ton of weight to the load we must carry.

Whether seeking an ass' load or an oxen's load, melanin adds weight and a considerable amount to whatever must be pulled. That being said, consider this reality when seeking your mate. Date who you want to date. Love who you want to love, but when preparing to tether, make sure that person you are tethering to has the load-bearing capacity to sustain a long-term relationship with you that includes an adjustment for melanin.

Understand when you hear someone speak about Black Love, he or she is talking about a very specific love, a tried-and-true love, a long-suffering love. Black love is a love that has had to kick down every societal barrier to exist. Black love should not be forsaken, nor taken for granted as it is too precious. Black love should be honored and cherished and so it lasts, yoke up with your equal.

Chapter 4: Progression-Growth Together

I'm a movement by myself, but I'm a force when we're together. I'm good all by myself, but baby you, you make me better... Words all couples should live by.

My mother was born in 1940, a time when blacks were still not permitted to dine in certain restaurants or drink out of certain fountains. Despite the skin that she was in and the many obstacles stacked against her, she secured a job with the Cincinnati Health Department, working her way through the ranks to become the right hand to the Health Commissioner. She retired at the tender young age of fifty-one and settled very nicely into her life of leisure, never looking back.

Part of the reason she could retire at such a young age and live so comfortably after retirement is that she had an amazing partner who understood from day one what my mom expected out of life. Not only did he understand what she wanted out of life, but he also appreciated what she wanted out of life. He was not intimidated by those expectations. He did not reject those expectations. He was all in, and he demonstrated that from the beginning.

When my dad first proposed to my mom, she said, "No." She told him that when he came back to her with the deed and keys to their own home, then and only then would she accept his ring and say, "I do." So, my dad did just that. He left, secured the bag, and returned to my mom with the deed and keys to their new home. They passed on a big wedding, opting instead for the Justice of the Peace. They settled down in their new four-bedroom, two-bathroom house with plenty of room to grow a family and built a beautiful life and legacy together.

See, my mom was a strong believer in progress. She was an overachiever. She was top of her class. She received stellar performance reviews at work. She cooked four-course meals every night, despite working a nine-to-five and toting kids around throughout the day. My mom was and still is amazing, but what impresses me most about my mom is that she always knew and understood her worth.

My mom knew and understood that what she brought to the table was valuable. Furthermore, she knew what she wanted out of life and was dead set on getting it. Consequently, anyone who wanted to be with her would work for her and then continue to work thereafter with her to obtain the life she wanted to live. She required of her mate someone who could and would add to her, making her trek uphill that much easier. That's the person she chose to marry. That's the person she wanted me to marry.

One of my mother's favorite lines was this. *"If he can't take you from an apartment to a house, or a house to a mansion, what is he good for?"*

Now, at first glance, one might assume this was a line befitting a gold digger, a name my mom would accept with pride because to whom much is given, much is required. Believe you, me. She was much, and she knew it. Yet and still, this is not at all about gold-digging. This mantra is about progress.

See, I heard that line from the time I started liking boys through today. So, when I experienced puppy love for the first time, I understood looks weren't everything. When I started having sex, I understood sex wasn't everything. When I first fell in love, I understood love wasn't everything. I was to expect and demand progress.

Progression is defined as the process of developing or moving gradually toward a more advanced state (*Oxford Languages*). What my mother meant to, and was successful in instilling in me, was that a mate worth yoking to will advance you forward. He will add to your plate rather than take away from it.

My mother instructed me to be with someone who would help me to the finish line, rather than be the hurdle at every pass. I was to be with someone I could progress through life with, not remain stagnant or still. Though progress can be a scary thing for many people and for various reasons.

Progress not only requires work, but it also requires change. So, before choosing a mate, one must consider that not everyone wants a heavier workload, and not everyone desires change.

Some reject progress because more will be expected of them, and they have no desire to work any harder than they are already. To that individual, progress will not be welcomed. Some reject progress because progress requires change; change in thought processes, change in habits, change in routine, change in direction, change in responsibility, all unknown variables. To progress, one must journey outside his or her comfort zone to an unfamiliar location he or she has never been, doing unfamiliar tasks he or she has never done. This is overwhelming for many.

Some fear progress for fear of failure and are crippled by the thought of not succeeding. They would rather not try at all than to try and fail.

Some people really are content with just getting by. They don't want much or require much.

On the flip side, you have folk like me who will die thinking they made it, because they never stopped pressing toward a mark that is further than where they lay. I fear not knowing success much more than I fear failing.

Now you tell me. How can the one who fears progress co-exist in a union with the one who fears stagnation?

Male Perspective

I'm a movement by myself, but I'm a force when we're together. Mommy I'm good all by myself, but baby you, you make me better... Words every couple should live by.

When I set out to find my wife, I knew it would take an incredibly special someone to be able to deal with me and help to continue to propel me to higher heights. Let me explain.

So, here I am, this big promoter, one of the biggest in Ohio. I threw parties, concerts, produced videos and productions... In short, I entertained for a living. We all know the life, or should I say, the perceived life of a male entertainer. We are viewed as living fast lives, consisting of multiple women, lots of alcohol, and fast money. For many, this is true. For me, not so much.

Now, I won't pretend I didn't have my fun. Monogamy was not always my bag, but neither was lying and cheating.

In my heyday, I was always about business first, and because I was concerned with business first, I made a point to protect it. This meant I couldn't lay down with anyone because "anyone" did not have my best interest at hand. I had no desire to be tethered to someone for eighteen years or more, simply because I could not control my member, so I controlled it. I had my fun but with limits.

Never would you find me popping bottles and walking around my events drunk because I needed my wits about me. I had arenas full of people depending on me to provide a safe environment where people could have fun. So, I always had to be ready to mitigate unwanted circumstances. I was also networking. I was attracting and meeting people who could get me in rooms I had yet to be in, so I had to be on my ish.

I worked too hard for my money to consider it fast, and I was not about to blow it on bull. I was reinvesting and reinventing. So, at the end of the night, in the wee hours of the morning when it was all said and done, I wanted nothing more than to retreat to a beautiful home where I would find my wife and child resting peacefully.

I pictured myself entering my home, peeking in at my child, kissing him or her on the forehead lightly so as not to wake them before making my way to my bedroom. Upon entry, I would find my rib sleeping ever so peacefully, not at all worried about who I was with after the club or why I was five minutes later than expected. No, she'd be there resting peacefully, so confident in herself and in us, knowing I only have eyes for her. If I'm lucky, she wakes up as I enter the room, ready to put me to bed the way only she knows how.

This is what I longed for. This is what I had to wait patiently for because anything less would impede progress and do more harm than good. So, I waited. I waited for the one God sent for me who had a life of her own, goals of her own, dreams of her own. I waited for the one who was too busy doing her to be bothered by me doing me. Instead, we would celebrate each other doing each other, together.

Now, before my wife and I got engaged, we had to have a coming to Jesus moment. Quite honestly, I fear this is a step many bypass and a major reason marriages fail. A coming to Jesus moment is where you come naked before each other. This is mask off, no play. This is where it gets really real. You tell each other the truth about where you want your life together to go.

Now, to be yoked to someone does not mean you become Siamese twins. If you two are blessed to be in the same field and form a partnership and work together, that's fine. That's great, but in no way am I saying the two have to be joined at the hip. What does have to happen, though, is that you have to outline your values and your goals, and they should align or complement. Then together you must decide your expectations for your future.

Now there is no way for you to know 100% what city you want to live in ten years from now, or what house you desire, because as your needs change, so will your living arrangements. However, what you need to discuss are the desired levels of progression and how you will reach those milestones together.

I was listening to TD Jakes, and he said something that really resonated in my spirit. He said, *"Investment breeds expectation."* Investment breeds expectation. So, what do you expect? Do you expect to stand still, or do you expect to progress? If progress is your goal, you must do the following.

Make sure you choose a progressive mate. Otherwise, you set your relationship up for failure and yourself, a lifetime of resentment.

Make sure your destinations align or, at the very least, compliment the other. Failing to do so will inevitably lead to roadblocks and pitfalls that would not otherwise exist.

Be each other's sounding boards more oft than not being transparent with needs and wants.

Be committed to supporting one another and committed to keeping the scales balanced as you propel one another forward together.

Finally, buckle up for the ride, and be sure to enjoy the journey and each other along the way.

Chapter 5: Sex

Female Perspective

Let's talk about sex baby!

I believe this to be common knowledge. However, if you are hiding under a rock and missed the memo, let it be known. Sex as an act of love for a woman begins in the mind, not in her pants. I repeat. Sex as an act of love for a woman begins in her mind.

To all my man dingo warriors who believe all you need is a third arm to win over a woman, you are literally missing the mark. You, kind sir, are a bootie call, something to pass the time, or an obligation, nothing more.

When the mind is not seduced, black women can and will compartmentalize sex and be the savage you never thought we could. Now, since we are talking about Black Love, I will assume we are all past this point and that this epiphany warrants no more than a friendly reminder. So, now we can get down to business.

Sex, or to be specific, sexual intercourse is defined as sexual contact between individuals involving penetration, especially the insertion of a man's erect penis into a woman's vagina, typically culminating in orgasm and the ejaculation of semen (*Oxford Languages*). Now, this is a sterile and extremely limited, loveless definition of sex.

Psychology Today expounds upon this definition and adds a little more substance concurring that for women, sex begins in the mind and is about being desired but can be a mixed bag that can easily become a daunting chore due to exhaustion- mental, physical, and emotional. Other sources depict sex as an exchange of energies and deposit of spirit, which really runs deep.

The Bible defines sex as a union, a union in which man and woman become one. So, what is sex for the sake of Black Love? With all definitions considered, I have constructed a working description that captures the essence of what sex is as it pertains to Black Love. Sex as an expression of love involves the intertwining of mind, body, and spirit resulting in mental stimulation, physical gratification, and emotional bonding, thus inciting an internal orgasmic climax that manifests externally through the ejaculation of semen and or female flooding, more commonly known as WAP.

So, why is sex important in a marital relationship and particularly to Black Love? Sex is essential to a marital relationship for a great deal of reasons. WebMD lists several health benefits — a happy immune system, increased libido in women, and improved bladder control in women. WebMD further claims sex lowers blood pressure, is good exercise, lowers heart attack risk, lessens pain, improves sleep, and eases stress.

While various studies support these claims, and I see clearly how each of these is paramount to the health and wellness of the individuals involved in the relationship, this does not give me what I'm looking for. These factors do little to sustain the relationship, besides giving people more time to be together because of the health benefits. What I wish to explore is sex as a sustainability factor.

I ran across an article in which Anik Debrot of Lausanne and her colleagues conducted studies that revealed that not the act of sex but the affection that accompanies sexuality contributes immensely to the satisfaction, the wellness and the sustainability of a relationship (*Krauss Whitbourne*, 2017). The Debrot team concluded that sex was "not only beneficial because of physiological or hedonic effects but because it promotes a stronger and more positive connection with the partner." It alleged that "When one person draws emotional benefits from sex, their partner's relationship satisfaction is also promoted over time."

Now, we're getting somewhere. This makes sense to me. When we consider connection, the thing God intended, we're stepping beyond the physical into the mental and spiritual aspects of sex, aligning ourselves with Word. Herein lies the blueprint for sex as an act of love.

One of the Bible's most compelling love stories is about the courtship between King Solomon and his Shulamite bride, the woman that pursued him and whom he pursued for love. Since the Bible informs us these two individuals were black, what better way to explore sex as it pertains to Black Love? Now, as we begin, a few things should be considered.

The Bible tells us of a Shulamite woman who longed for King Solomon. He was the one her soul loveth. This desire began before she had ever been touched by this man. This desire began in the depths of this woman's imagination and resonated to her soul, for she knew him not and was a virgin at the beginning of this tale.

At the same time, boasting of her unrivaled beauty, the Shulamite woman implored acceptance of her darker skin. Does this sound familiar? Does this sound like colorism doing what colorism does best? Colorism separates, distinguishes, and dictates desirable vs. undesirable, and this is something that black women in America, no matter how beautiful, wrestle with daily. It plagues one's psyche and often renders a woman insecure despite what she reveals for show or, as we say nowadays, for the gram. The fact that the Shulamite addresses her blackness at all lets the reader know this is truly an uncertainty for her that requires acquiescence.

King Solomon had many, many wives, which scholars believe he married for various reasons, be it power, control, or expansion. While customary for a king to take several wives, Solomon's were deemed somewhat excessive, at times inexplicable, and this too was believed to be a discouragement for the Shulamite woman because she sincerely loved this man. Consequently, Solomon had his work cut out for him, but because this was the woman he would marry for love, he was ready to put in this work.

Now, King Solomon was a powerful king renowned for his wisdom, which he sought directly from God. This wisdom is displayed in his management of his Shulamite bride. In the passage leading to their union, we find all the components necessary to open this woman, this virgin woman up, making her succumb to her true love and one desire.

Solomon leads with compliments, telling the Shulamite the joints of her thighs are like jewels, the work of the hands of a cunning workman. He likened her breasts to two fawns and her eyes to beautiful pools, crystal clear and full of life.

Solomon continues to adulate this woman, thus making love to her mind first. He then tells her what he will do to her, arousing her physically and seducing her body with every word. He likens her stature unto a palm tree and her breasts to clusters of grapes, which he will climb and take hold of. Ain't that a panty dropper?

Lastly, and perhaps most important, he adorns her above all others, describing her mouth as the best wine. This is the acceptance of who she is as well the assurance of her place in his heart that she so longed for. In other words, this was the coup de gras, and what she needed, to know she was safe to submit.

By these seamless acts, this black woman is convinced and proudly proclaims, I am my beloved's, and his desire is toward me. Then she tells him, *"Come, my beloved, let us go forth..."* Translation: In my best Marvin Gaye voice, "Let's get it on."

Male Perspective

Let's talk about sex baby!

I believe this to be common knowledge. However, if you are hiding under a rock and missed the memo, let it be known. Sex does not constitute love for a man. I repeat. Sex does not constitute love for a man. Sex in a man does indeed begin in his pants.

To all my beautiful, misled sistas who believe that because a man laid down with you, he is infatuated and yours for the taking, you are mistaken. Please let actions other than sex dictate a man's feelings for you. If you choose to ignore my advice, you are setting yourself up for a major let down.

When a man lays down nothing but pipe to please a woman... Let me rephrase. When all a man is required to do is lay down pipe to please a woman, then that is all he will do. That woman becomes nothing more than an easy lay, and the man acts out his savage ways as accepted and expected in this savage society in which we dwell.

Now, since we are talking about Black Love, I will assume we are all past this point and that this epiphany warrants no more than a friendly reminder. So, now we can get down to business.

Psychologists and therapists alike concur that for a man, sex begins in the body. Furthermore, they attest to sex being a hunger fueled by testosterone. It's the burst of adrenaline craved, supplying much-needed energy and excitement, and, with these claims, I agree.

Psychology Today, however, goes so far as to still constitute sex as an act of love claiming that a man's strongest desire is to please his mate, and when he ejaculates, he feels like he is home, rendering him vulnerable and more susceptible to love. Here, I beg to differ.

While I agree men often have a strong desire to please a woman, rarely is it about the woman. More often than not, this desire stems from his desire to be "the man." No doubt a man wants to leave an impression that keeps a woman open, that makes her brag to her friends and have flashback orgasms in the shower, but what does that have to do with love?

When a man ejaculates, truth be told, his soldiers have found their way to a home, be it a hot air balloon, a canal, vivacious mound… you get my point, but that does not constitute home for his heart. So, the vulnerability of the man lasts about as long as the orgasm. When he is finished, he can detach mentally, physically, emotionally and keep it moving on to the next conquest. When sex is an act of love, the man will not just arouse the woman's body. He will be mindful of his woman and awaken her spirit as Solomon did his Shulamite. He will truly see her.

See, black people in America share inescapable trial and tribulation that depletes us. When a black man loves a black woman and employs sex as an act of love, as the head… as the king, he will do those things Solomon did to prep his queen and free her from the spoils of a society that did not, does not, and will not appreciate her. He will give her a place of peace mentally, a spiritual bond that replenishes her emotionally, the assurance she needs to feel safe, and then he will pleasure her physically, in ways she never imagined.

This black man will do so knowing full well that these are the keys to unlock passions and desires in a woman making her free to fully submit to him mind, body, and soul. He will have no regrets, no reservations, and no hesitation because he wants to do that for the woman he will marry for love.

No question, the Shulamite woman was everything King Solomon wanted, needed, and more because he allowed her to be that to him by freeing her of her inhibition. I believe Solomon to be the wise king of old who drew wisdom directly from God and am convinced this is the blueprint for sex as it pertains to Black Love.

Chapter 6: Kids

Female Perspective

I remember, like yesterday, the moment they placed my baby in my arms for the first time. She had beautiful mocha skin and silky black hair. Her cries were the sweetest song I had ever heard and those eyes... They were the most beautiful eyes I had ever seen, and in them existed my entire world. This magnificent and overwhelming feeling subdued me. In that moment, I knew I would lay down my life a million times over to never see harm come her way. She was my morning sun, my cup of tea; my shining star; the best of me.

For months, I could not take my eyes off her. I remember sitting in the pediatrician's office for her checkup and hearing a voice say jokingly, "Girl, you are going to stare the black off that child." Believe me, she was not lying. If staring the black off your child was a person, that was me. I was obsessed with my child. In my best Stevie Wonder voice, I was overjoyed over love over her. How could I not be?

I carried this child inside me for nine months. I felt a seed grow into an embryo and an embryo into a fetus. I felt her arms and legs flailing inside me, her body contorting at the sound of her mother's voice. I was her lifeline. I was her sustenance, her energy, her immunity, her shelter, her protection. For nine months, I was her everything; and that did not change when she was extracted from my body.

God had bestowed upon me a miraculous blessing, and with that, the greatest of responsibilities that I dare not take for granted. Especially for a single parent like myself, with this type of assignment on her shoulders, it's no wonder how children can inflict significant strain on romantic relationships.

Children require a great deal of time, energy, effort, money, and patience, and what tends to happen is we divest so much of that into our children that we have nothing left for our spouse or significant other. This is not done maliciously or intentionally. It just happens because a child, until able to stand on his or her own, needs this and more from you. Nonetheless, it isn't fair; and what we have to figure out is how to be everything to our children without losing sight of our mate. One way to accomplish this is through shared management.

Shared management of children helps to keep clear the line of sight to your mate. It has somewhat of a domino effect on a relationship, not only promoting solidarity but making possible increased quality time, which is one of the pillars of a successful union. Shared management mitigates the chance of one party in the relationship feeling alone in a situation that the two of them created and eventually resenting the other for it. When the two share the responsibility of raising their children equally, a bond is forged, and a mutual respect ensues that fortifies a relationship.

Shared management makes possible time together, a necessary component in the cultivation of a long-lasting and healthy relationship. Whether that time together is spent dancing the night away and capping it off with passionate sex because you both shared in the responsibility, and neither of you had to exhaust yourselves, or whether that time is spent passed out in each other's arms because the kids wore both of you out; you are in it together, and together, makes the difference.

The fact of the matter is shared management is crucial because raising children is arguably the most challenging job on earth. To think that one can and or should be the sole manager of such a task is unreasonable and inequitable. Unfortunately, because we do not live in a perfect world, at times, it's also unavoidable.

So many variables factor into this equation, including breastfeeding, employment, finances, couple's status, living arrangements…The list goes on and on. Consequently, everyone does not have the opportunity to subscribe to the shared management plan, and the burden of child-rearing may, in many instances, weigh more on one parent than the other. When this occurs, grace must enter in.

Be clear. Grace is not the nanny's name. Grace is not granny. No! Grace is another instrument that keeps clear the line of sight to your mate by forcing you to see them. Grace demands that you recognize the impact the kids are having on your mate; that you notice when she's depleted and understand why; that you notice what she needs to rejuvenate; that you notice where you can brace the impact. Grace requires you to be present and aware and engaged and thoughtful. Grace is understanding and forgiveness, and mercy without question.

Grace means rather than become disgruntled because your mate is too tired for you after dealing with her kids all day, you tell her not to cook and surprise the family with dinner, instead. Grace is arranging for the kids to go to Auntie's house and surprising your mate with three days of rest, relaxation, intimacy, and sex. Grace is knowing that until you can lighten the load by altering your schedule and behaviors and habits, you have no right to be mad because when you wed a person with children, yours or otherwise, that load falls on both parties' shoulders in one way or another. You are in it together, and your mate's contribution to carry should be valued and appreciated and certainly not undermined or taken for granted.

Male Perspective

I don't know if it was shock or amazement. It was probably a combination of the two. Whatever the case, I was mesmerized. I could not turn away from this miracle taking place right before my eyes. As this precious creature that I love so much emerged from this precious creature I loved so much, I knew my world would never be the same.

"Mr. Young, would you like to hold your baby? Mr. Young?"

Rarely was I speechless, but in that moment, I was frozen in time.

"I'm so sorry. Yes! Please! Give me my baby!"

The nurse fixed my arms in the cradling position, cautioned me of her head, and then placed the most beautiful thing I had ever laid eyes on in my arms. She had smooth caramel skin and curly, black hair. She was so tiny. Her little, delicate body fit inside one of my hands. All I could think as I gazed upon her was, *Oh my god! Is she really mine?*

I knew in that very moment I would lay down my life a million times over to never see her want for anything. She was daddy's little princess, and daddy would love and protect her at all cost. I would give her the moon, the stars, and everything in between.

As for my queen, not only did she bless me with my princess, but she gifted me with two princes. My baby came into this world with two big brothers to help me look after her and her mom, and I was honored and eager to make sure all of us lived happily ever after.

See, I have a blended family, and a blended family can be quite complicated. Still, the key to blending successfully and with the least amount of resistance is controlling the one thing you can control — yourself. Control how you respond to situations. Be more proactive than reactive. Know that when you marry a mother, you are marrying a package, and whether or not you are accepted as a dad, you are family.

You must work diligently with your mate to carve out the space in which you dwell that best serves all parties. So how do we accomplish this?

Like always, communication is key. Talk to your mate. Ask her for a clear picture of the current situation. For example, is dad estranged, or is he present? How is co-parenting working out? Who is responsible for what? What is the expectation of how you are to interact with the kids? Discovery must take place.

Don't expect the children to fall in love with the "enemy" overnight. Just because you and your mate have gotten acclimated to the situation doesn't mean that the children have, especially considering they are typically not introduced on the front end of the journey. We, as parents, are protective of our kids and rarely involve them until we are confident that he or she is "the one." So while we may have had years to fall in love, the kids may have only had months. You must be mindful of this. If it took the two parties who welcomed the relationship years to fall in love, how much longer will it take those to fall who may see this as a gross imposition? Allow a relationship to grow organically.

Like Steve Harvey recommends in *Think Like a Man*, introduce your mate to your kids the moment you know you are working toward forever. Find common ground and create opportunities for the kids and your mate to become familiar in informal and less invasive settings. Try some team-building exercises to develop trust. Have air guitar and karaoke battles where the kids and the mate team up, and if you're really evolved and the opportunity presents, include the biological parent. Allow them to help their children through this transition and to help you win their trust by issuing their stamp of approval. When raising kids, there is no blueprint, and we need all the help we can get. It truly does take a village to raise a child. Create that harmonious village to cultivate health and strength in a blended family.

Managing blended families like biological families takes a great deal of time, effort, and energy while walking on eggshells in a field of landmines at the same time. Tension can flare at any given moment because additional external variables add influence. Failing to understand and or not take personal the challenges associated with blending families can wreak all kinds of havoc on a relationship. Don't let it.

Love and patience will be your greatest weapons in this battle. Use them as often as possible. This does not mean one is expected to take unnecessary abuse. Boundaries have to be established for all, kids included, but be cognizant of the delicacy of the situation and the vulnerabilities the children are faced with. Move accordingly and do the best you can do as a unit, and in due time, you will win together.

Female Perspective

I don't know that anyone, male or female, can brace for the impact a child will have on his or her life. It's as if a complete shift in the universe occurs, and the sun is no longer the center. Children cause parents to move differently, think different, worry differently, hustle differently. You love differently, and as long as you are doing all of these things in sync and on one accord, your romantic relationship does not have to suffer.

Therefore, equally paramount to raising kids in a relationship is that in the beginning, it started with being equally yoked so that differences in values, beliefs, and systems do not pose an added threat to an already difficult task. As previously stated, being equally yoked does not assume that you and your mate agree on everything.

However, equally yoked suggests that your beliefs and value systems are complementary and can be congruently interconnected.

Then you have the middle. In the middle you have transparency by way of effective and continuous communication throughout your relationship. Remember, as you grow and evolve, so will your thoughts, needs, and wants. Failing to disclose these nuances as that evolution occurs will place you miles away from your mate simply because you did not tell him or her where you were going and neglected to invite them along for the ride.

Distance and unawareness cause discord and allows for asynchronous government. Asynchronous government leads to infighting that can turn to war. Like we see in our country today, asynchronous government can tear a family to shreds quicker than any weapon and should be avoided by all means necessary, and in this case, all means are quite simple. Just talk it out.

Male Perspective

Lastly, at the end of the raising kids in a relationship challenge, is commitment. Nothing in life operates by happenstance. This is no different. Being successful in child-rearing as a couple without injuring the relationship is a choice that requires dedication to the cause and is an obligation that, as *Oxford Languages* so eloquently puts, restricts freedom of action. Commit to not allowing yourself to act as if you are the only one who matters in this equation. Commit to working as a team. Commit to moving as one entity. Commit to respecting all parties' boundaries and responding accordingly. Commit to not abandoning ship even when the winds and waves prove themselves a vehement force of nature.

When those tumultuous times come, which occur at any given moment but certainly around age fourteen, right around the time they are "grown" and start smelling themselves, grab tighter the helm, working hand in hand with your mate to steer your ship to safety and calmer shores.

Chapter 7: Friends First

Female Perspective

For years, a popular ice breaker and cliche, designed to give you a glimpse into who a person was, came in the form of a hypothetical question. That question was, if you were shipwrecked on a deserted island and could be with anyone on earth, who would it be? Not until 2020 did this hypothetical question become a reality, and not until 2020 did we realize the importance of that answer having been my significant other and best friend.

With the onset of COVID-19, men and women everywhere found themselves stranded on a deserted island. Only, we did not get to pick some famous celebrity or blast from the past, with whom we'd be shipwrecked. Instead, we landed on that island with our significant others. Unfortunately, many of us, throughout this journey, are discovering that our shipmates... our co-captains in life are more foe than friend. Couples who have been together for years are learning the hard way they are incompatible with their mates and that they really dislike one another but had gotten used to tolerating each other. No wonder domestic violence has spiked all over the world.

This phenomenon, though horrible at best, causes me to reflect on a hilarious episode of *Martin*, in which the self-proclaimed "Love Doctor" Martin Payne, gives his guests, The Bookers, the following advice.

"You got to be friends first. I say you got to be friends first."

If nothing more, COVID-19 has undoubtedly validated the Love Doctor's prescription. Let's explore.

The Bible tells us friendship requires you to stick close like a brother, to love at all times, to show yourself friendly, and to stand with the other against opposition. On the flip side, the Bible warns us mere companionship can bring ruins. I bring this to your attention because our current condition indicates that couples today, intentionally or not, have opted for companionship rather than friendship, and men and women alike are no doubt suffering as a result. Therefore, when seeking a long-lasting and healthy relationship, paramount to its success, is distinguishing between the two because only one is suited to last and to endure the tests of time.

Let's compare.

If a friend sticks closer than a brother, the flight risk, also known as break up or divorce, is mitigated. When adhering to the notion of sticking closer than a brother, arguments, for example, hit differently. What I mean is, inevitable is a dispute between siblings, right? Siblings live in close quarters. They see each other daily and, by default, have more opportunity for disagreement. Disagreements between siblings are considered natural and are expected, as a result, and not the end of the world. No dispute can stop a sister from being a sister. You share a bloodline. It is what it is.

When looking at a romantic relationship on those terms, because you are friends first, the same becomes true of that bond. Arguments become less detrimental, and life-altering and no dispute stop you from being what you are to one another, be it spouse, life partner, or significant other. Friendship becomes the bloodline that allows us to remain who we are to each other. Unrealistic is the notion that you can be with someone day in and day out and never disagree, no matter the relation. Yet, some people will die alone because they have this fairy tale ideology that this is supposed to be true of a romantic relationship, but who can live up to that?

That being said, just like we might say of our siblings after a spat, "they will be alright" so can be the case with our mate. Only, instead of "they will," it becomes "we will." "We will be alright." It's only a difference of opinion, and because we are friends and share that friendship bloodline, we do not have to jump ship. Instead, we can find a compromise and meet in the middle. Or we can agree to disagree and move past it. Regardless, this approach allows us to see more often than not that whatever we are arguing about is just not that serious. If given the opportunity, it too shall pass because our bloodline, aka friendship, is too valuable for it not to. We can stay who we are to each other because we are friends first.

Friendship is commanded to love at all times and show itself friendly. So, when you are friends first, love is the tactical force motivating and driving the relationship as opposed to narcissism or personal gain. Love actions prevail in friendship. When love actions prevail, relationships are sustained, spiritual connections are reinforced, and growth is facilitated.

A general desire for the other's well-being is prominent in friendship. Friends administer kindness and mercy and grace instead of spite and contempt. It's a whole different vibe where selflessness rather than selfishness abounds, and it's ok. Expect the reciprocal because we are friends first.

Friendship demands you face off together, not against one another. Bonnie and Clyde were friends. Thomasine and Bushrod were friends. Queen and Slim developed a friendship almost overnight because they chose to do so. See, two of these couples cited may be fictitious characters, but all demonstrate a very real concept. Couples who are friends first stand together and fight together against any and all odds.

So, when that home wrecking woman decides to assert herself, she is not met with opposing force by the woman only. No, she is rejected and ejected by the man she is in pursuit of, because that man is your friend, first. He has an obligation to stand with you. When that home wrecking man asks the question from the popular 90s hit, "What's Your Man Got To Do With Me?" You have answers for days because you dare not disrespect your friend, nor will you allow him to do so. You honor your obligation to your friend. And when something as unfamiliar and severe as COVID hits, you are working together to make this very harsh reality easier for one another. You do not compile it. You counter it and become the other's peace amid a turbulent storm because that's what friends are for.

The Bible tells us, *"Two are better than one… for if they fall, the one will lift up his fellow."* This is only required of a friend. Friends have responsibilities and accountability to one another. A companion, however, has no obligation, no demands, no requirements except to be there. In fact, the Bible warns a man who hath many companions may come to ruin. If you are not experiencing a bond closer than a brother, a relationship-driven by love actions and a soldier marching by your side … your shipmate is a companion, and you best beware.

Male Perspective

I will be honest with you. I've had my fair share of companions, really great ones, and my experience was not consistent with what the Bible said about companions bringing a man to ruins. On the contrary, mine was determined to win me over. My companions did everything for me. They cooked for me, cleaned for me, rubbed my back, washed my clothes… Whatever I asked, it didn't matter. They were down for me. They spoiled me… They spoiled me…

Wait a minute! Spoil and ruin are synonyms, are they not? See, when I initially read that verse, I thought in terms of the companion inflicting external ruin on the man. And while this can be and is the case in many situations, this was not the case in mine. The ruin didn't come from my companions doing something to me or against me. They were great! No... The ruin came internally by way of them enabling me. I was not held accountable in my relationships. I did what I wanted to do. There was no demand or desire for me to be better. There was no discomfort, no stretching, no pulling, and by default, no room for growth. For a man, especially in this day, this is the worst type of ruin. This is the type of ruin that cultivates self-destruction.

But then... like King Solomon, I met my Shulamite bride, the one I would love. She challenged everything I thought I knew about myself, from my desire to have kids to my favorite pastime. We talked about anything and shared everything. We took time to actually learn one another and enjoy one another and really developed an affinity for being in one another's presence. We became friends first, and because we were friends, I never wanted to hurt her. You don't hurt your friends, right?

For years I was told a man doesn't know what kind of man he is until he knows what kind of woman he wants. I never agreed with this statement until this point in my life.

See, unlike with my companions, I wanted to be better with my Shulamite. I wanted to keep my bride. She really mattered to me. So, I decided what man I wanted to be. I decided what man I wanted to give to her... a man who would honor and protect all that she is. A man who would love and cherish the extensions of herself that she so graciously blessed me with, my two sons. A man who would forever be indebted to her for the greatest gift she could give me, my seed, my daughter. A man who would forever and ever and ever be her friend. I might not be walking in my purpose right now had we not become friends first.

Female Perspective

I feel you. In 2021, I will marry my friend. What's so crazy is that I have literally known this man my whole life. His sister and my sister were best friends, and because of that friendship bloodline, I always considered him family.

As young adults, we worked in complementing fields. Since we were family, we partnered on a lot of things together. As a result of us becoming partners, we saw much more of each other with our weekly check-ins and lunches. We attended different networking events together, and we always had fun. We worked well together.

Eventually, we started hanging outside of work, being that we shared many of the same interests. For example, he rode motorcycles, and I enjoyed riding on the back of motorcycles. So, sometimes we'd just ride, no particular place to go but just enjoying each other and the wind. We played well together.

Despite there being a very natural connection and or attraction, we never broached the subject. In fact, we each went on to marry others and just continued as family. Then, one day, I left the corporate world and made a career change that landed me in his lane, and there was no question who I was going to work with. Of course, I joined his team. He was family. Now, at this point, I had been divorced for years. He had been divorced for months. Who but God knew the perfect storm was brewing?

One day, we attended a meeting together during which time, he was recognized, but not for his real estate business. He was recognized for his extracurricular activity, which was the successful completion of an IronMan race. If you're not familiar with what that is, it's a triathlon that athletes all over the world travel to complete. In this race, he was required to run thirty miles, bike one-hundred-twelve miles, and swim six miles all in one setting. Now, I always knew I was the rib to a superhero, but I had no clue he had been there all along.

See, my heart's desire was that God sends me a man who could and would elevate me as much as I, him. I wanted a man whose drive matched or exceeded my drive...someone who could show me something new. As they continued to speak on his accomplishments in that meeting, I was intrigued, to say the least. I thought to myself, *Bingo*!

Soon thereafter, he asked me to join him on his boat one summer evening, where we had a real conversation about where we were in life and what we wanted in a relationship. We were both very transparent and honest. I will admit I was disappointed to find we were in two different places. I was ready for a committed relationship. He was not, but I understood why. While my mind told me, *"That's your cue to exit stage left*", my heart told me otherwise. My heart said, *"You belong to him."* So, I took a leap of faith and popped the question.

"Do you want me to wait for you?"

He responded with a resounding, "Yes, absolutely!"

Four years later, here we are, preparing to jump the broom. Now that may seem like a long time, and it definitely was for me, until I realized… Had we crossed that line any sooner, fiancé would have been part of my past and not my purpose. Yes, we were family. Yes, we were partners. Yes, we were companions, but we needed that four-year incubation period to become friends. We needed that time to discover one another, to learn one another, and to stretch one another.

My fiancé would always tell me… I don't want to mess us up. I have to work on myself. I was his Shulamite bride, the one whom he would love, and not until he knew he had become the man he wanted to be for me did he present himself… I was his friend, first; and now that we are friends first, we can live out our purpose with God in tow as that three-cord strand that will not be broken.

Chapter: 8 What About Your Friends?

Female Perspective

The time had finally come for Antoinette to reveal a painful secret to her best friend, Sharon. Months of counseling, months of fighting, and months of crying, unfortunately, had not yielded the reward Antoinette so desperately longed for. Her marriage had come to its demise. Antoinette was filing for divorce, and while she had prepared to deliver this unfortunate news to Sharon, she was in no way prepared for her response. Sharon's response was far from what one might expect.

She did not respond with, "Good! You didn't need him, anyway." Nor did she hit her with, "I'm sorry. We'll get through this." Instead, Sharon replied, "Antoinette, when I sat in attendance at your wedding and touched and agreed, I made a vow to you and to God to do all I can to undergird your marriage. Therefore, I cannot and will not accept that your marriage is over until I have done all I can do to save it. Do you still love your husband?"

Antoinette replied, "Yes."

Sharon continued. "Do you want your marriage to work?"

Antoinette replied. "Yes."

Then, the coup de gras... Sharon asked, "May I speak with him?"

Antoinette replied, "If you choose to."

Sharon then set out on a mission to save her friend's marriage. Sharon met with Antoinette's husband. She counseled him. She prayed with him, and she encouraged him. Sharon continued the fight her friend no longer had the strength to carry on. When Sharon had finally been backed into the ropes, having taken blow after blow through actionless lip service, empty promises, disappointment, and denial, she realized there was no winning this fight and threw in the towel. Reluctantly, she conceded. Sharon was forced to return to her corner where Antoinette awaited, and having done all she could, Sharon gave Antoinette her blessing to divorce. She then cried with her friend. She prayed with her friend. She stood by her friend's side and nurtured her through the pain of divorce and the mourning after.

The Bible says, "*No greater love than this that a man lay down his life for a friend.*" When we hear this verse, our minds jump to Jesus and the cross and literal death. However, this very true story is yet another example of how a man lays down her life for a friend.

Sharon demonstrated the role of a friend in a relationship battle. This scenario was no different from bringing the Vaseline and the tennis shoes ready to go to war, except this meant so much more. See, Sharon was fighting for her friend's life. Antionette was losing half of herself, as she had become one with her husband. Rather than be a spectator or an enabler, Sharon chose to put herself to the side and devoted time, energy, effort, and emotion into bringing her friend back into herself.

Now, of course, Antoinette never needed Sharon's blessing to divorce. We know this, and for some, this may have been too much. Some might see this as invasive, and that's ok. I'm confident that is why Sharon asked permission before inserting herself into the situation. Nonetheless, no matter Antoinette's answer, be it yes or no, Sharon's actions, and her desire to jump in the fight, as well her vow to uphold their marriage, epitomized friendship and how a friend should move in support of a friend in a relationship.

Now, I would be remiss not to point out this move has contingencies. If a friend is in imminent danger, meaning a friend is being subjected to physical abuse, drug abuse, etc., this fight will look a lot different. However, since we are speaking on Black Love, I will trust we are past this point and able to push forward.

The Bible tells us, "*Two are better than one…For if they fall, the one will lift up his fellow*"

That being said…

Ladies! Friendship is so much more than having someone to gossip with or tear the club up with. Friendship comes with responsibility. The responsibility is to lift one another up. Then with responsibility comes expectation. The expectation is that we will be elevated by our friends, and the fact of the matter is, when we involve a third-party mate, the lift is subject to getting heavier. So, as the receiver of friendship while in a meaningful, long term relationship, the expectation is not that your bestie encourages you to leave your mate at the drop of a dime or that she continues to monopolize your time; or that she continues to set you up with dudes; or that she'll pop up on your mate unannounced when you're not there; or that she makes your mate uncomfortable with inappropriate actions or words…

The expectation is that your friend lifts you up by honoring your decision to be with this person who makes you better and that she honors that decision by respecting that relationship. This means your friend may have to help to renew your strength a time or two when love has worn you out, but also what this means is there are clear boundaries that don't get breached and clear lines that don't get crossed. To accept anything less of your friend is a disservice to your friendship and your relationship.

Male Perspective

Todd, as he approached his one-year anniversary, reflected on the last year of his life as a married man. His mind journeyed back to his bachelor party, which he remembered like yesterday. Ok now, get your mind out of the gutter. Todd was not reflecting upon all the beautiful women surrounding him at the party. He was not reflecting on his last romp as a single man because no romping took place. He reflected on the friend, and I use the term lightly, the friend he lost that day.

See, Aaron had been a problem for Todd's wife Christine from the day she and Todd became exclusive. However, until the day of his bachelor party, Todd viewed Aaron's behavior as "boys being boys." Now, granted, he was never disrespectful in terms of insulting Christine or calling her out of her name; but what he did wasn't much better.

Aaron brought a different woman to every event Chris and Todd hosted and to every double date. He made a habit of putting his callers on speaker before he and Todd would head out for a night on the town, and of course, those callers were always female and always plural; and Aaron always said, "We are on our way."

Todd would most certainly assure Christine that Aaron was in no way referring to him as there were other male friends present. Nonetheless, Todd knew it still bothered her. Think about it, Men. How could it not? I don't know a person on earth who wasn't taught in some way, shape, form, or fashion, "Birds of a feather flock together." Yet despite that, Chris tolerated it and trusted Todd to do right by her, and for the next two years, that's exactly what he did. Then, he did a thing.

Todd mustered up enough courage to propose to Christine, and when he proposed, he did so in private. No lights, no camera, no fans, no Aarons were in attendance, just he and Christine.

Still, before responding to his proposal, with a resounding yes like Todd eagerly anticipated, Christine asked a question. "Are you sure you are through playing?"

Todd was confused as he had never cheated on Christine. He had never played with Christine. Truth be told, he was a goner day one. So, as he rose to his feet, he responded with his own question and asked, "Why would you say that? "

Christine's answer was simple but complex. "Because of the company you keep."

Todd replied. "What do you mean by that?"

Christine ran it down. "Baby, your best friend, is a womanizer. He is always trying to set you up with someone. He's always dragging you to the strip club. He makes a point every chance he gets to let me know I'm not safe by throwing your boys' night out shenanigans in my face. I've tolerated it as your girlfriend because aside from hanging with him, you've never given me a reason not to trust you. However, as a wife, this gives me pause because while boyfriend is a boy's role, husband is a man's role; and I don't understand how any man can be comfortable in that space. It's childish, and I'm too grown to subject myself to a lifetime of that."

Christine's words cut Todd like a knife. They were unexpected, but Todd could not say they were unwarranted. Sure, he knew Aaron was not Chris' cup of tea, but he had somehow rendered himself oblivious to the idea of her having such strong feelings about the situation. Todd took a deep breath. He returned to one knee. He looked deep into Chris' eyes and said, "I'm sorry. I should have recognized the degree to which my dealings with Aaron bothered you."

Todd, in the next breath, swore to Christine he would never let anyone come between them and that he would talk to Aaron. He assured her things would change. He promised Christine she was the only woman for him and that he would spend every waking moment proving that to her every day of her life if she would just be his wife.

Needless to say, Chris was blown away by Todd's proposal. In her heart of hearts, she believed him. So, when Todd popped open that

Cartier box, momentarily blinding Christine, the deal was done. The moment Todd eagerly anticipated had come.

Christine screamed at the top of her lungs that resounding, "Yes!" Todd so yearned to hear, as tears of joy poured from her eyes. She and Todd celebrated their engagement by dancing the rest of the night away, just the two of them, arm and arm, in the living room. The next day, Todd wondered how he would break the news to Aaron. Although he was so excited, he knew his friend might not share his sentiment and felt it might damage their friendship. He approached with caution, and just as Todd suspected, Aaron's reaction was one of disapproval.

Aaron berated Todd with asinine questions like, "Why are you willing to give up all this ass walking around? Are you marrying her because she is pregnant?"

Todd just sat in amazement. Never had he seen his friend's behavior as what it truly was, jealousy and envy. Todd's girl was the $#!/, and everyone knew it. In fact, every other friend of Todd's congratulated him and bragged on the one Todd bagged, but not Aaron. He was pissed. So before things got out of hand, Todd ended the conversation and decided to give Aaron a couple weeks to process and adjust.

The next time Todd and Aaron spoke, Aaron appeared to be accepting and supportive. Todd explained to Aaron, some behaviors had to change. Aaron agreed, and behaviors did change while in Christine's face. Aaron stopped bringing different women around. He stopped answering the phone on speaker and stopped moving in a manner that made Todd's fiancée uncomfortable. That is until they were outside of Christine's presence. When out and about, Aaron continued to parade women around Todd and encourage him to "just talk to them," as if he were doing Todd a favor. Aaron had yet to grasp the concept that his toxic behaviors had to change not just for Christine's sake but for Todd's. I think Big Pun said it best when he said, I don't want to be a player no more. Todd was indeed done playing, but his friend refused to get it.

As the wedding day approached, Todd chose his brother as the best man. The best man was in charge of two major things, the rings and the bachelor party. Aaron couldn't care less about the ring part, but where it came to the bachelor party, Aaron wanted in. He begged to help.

Todd knew Aaron would help put on a good show for the guys to enjoy, so, although reluctant, he agreed. But of course, Aaron went too far. Aaron hired a sexy stripper/masseuse known for happy endings and pushed her on Todd. Aaron then perched on Todd's shoulder like a devil, in his ear, encouraging him at every turn to bite the apple. He repeated over and over, "It's your last day as a free man. She'll never know."

If not for this behavior being consistent with Aaron's normal routine, Todd would have no doubt made yet another excuse for his friend, blaming his immoral actions on the alcohol and ignoring him like usual, but not this time. This time was different. Todd was embarking on one of the most important days of his life and was doing so, eyes wide open. Aaron was trying to sabotage his happiness. He could no longer make excuses for his so-called friend, who had no problem putting his marriage at risk.

Aaron had become a detriment to Todd because he refused to see Todd. He refused to understand Todd had grown into a man and wanted to remain the man he could look at in the mirror every day, with respect; a man whose wife felt secure and happy knowing her husband had put away childish things. For that reason, Todd was fed up and would no longer tolerate Aaron's behavior.

Todd asked Aaron to leave and to take his masseuse with him, but before doing so, Todd made sure Aaron knew not to show up to the wedding. Aaron honored Todd's wishes. When Christine asked why Todd's oldest friend was not there, he told her, "Because I am your man, and I choose you!"

Similar to their engagement night, Todd and Christine spent their wedding night, dancing the night away as if they were the only two people in the room. They haven't stopped dancing yet. Todd never regretted choosing his lifetime over his season and thanks God that he had the wherewithal to choose right and in the nick of time. While Todd indeed was a stand-up guy, the flesh can only take so much before it's weakened, and one moment of weakness can cost a man his entire life.

Fellas, the Bible says, "*Do not be deceived, bad company ruins good morals…*" for a reason. Take heed. Even iron wears thin, and at some point, that bad company will get you into bad company. So, don't get so full of yourself and high on your ability to exercise restraint that you put yourself in positions you have no business being, forsaking good judgment, to hang with a friend. A friend will not put you in those types of situations.

A friend's role is to encourage and undergird. When this ceases to happen like in Todd and Aaron's case, we must reevaluate that person's position in our lives, even when they've been there forever. The Bible says, "*A man of many companions may come to ruin*" So, paramount to a successful relationship is distinguishing between a companion and a friend and treating them accordingly before ruining what is important in your life.

A friend will honor your relationship and will see your relationship as a blessing rather than a curse. They will lift you and your mate up. A companion does not shoulder the same responsibility. A companion will weigh the load down that they are supposed to be hoisting. When you see this happening, recognize that is not your friend. This ability to discern between the two becomes even more crucial when dealing with opposite-sex friends.

Opposite-Sex Friends

Opposite-sex friends are tricky. You could have never in your life had a romantic desire for that person, but because of how men and women are programmed, your mate will feel some sense of uncertainty when the friend in question is the opposite sex. This feeling is normal. This feeling is understandable. This feeling is predictable. Consequently, you may have to work a little harder to show your mate that you and your opposite-sex friend are just that; and that's ok. The situation warrants extra.

Allow opportunity for them to become friends. Encourage it! Double date and split up so they can bond. Have game nights where they can be partners. Create space for them to get to know one another. Monitor their interaction a little closer. Your opposite-sex friend may easily overstep his or her bounds because of the dichotomy of male and female relationships. Be mindful of this and pay close attention. In addition, beware of attempting to introduce a new opposite-sex friend into an already established long-term romantic relationship.

Female Perspective

My mother told me the same opposite-sex friends you have going into a long-term relationship are the only opposite-sex friends you have any business having. I respect that. I understand that. I honor that because the alternative makes no sense. What justification is there for bringing a new opposite-sex friend into a relationship? How and why did you cross that bridge to intimacy to deem this person as such, when you already have all the opposite-sex friend you need on your arm. Now, if you choose to ignore the voice of wisdom and decide to journey down that slope, anyway, just know it's quite the slippery one and may put you at risk for more than you'd bargained.

If a new opposite sex friendship has to be introduced, tread lightly and with your mate in tow. Discuss first with your mate why the forging of this new friendship is important and necessary, and at the very least, give them an opportunity to participate. If, for any reason other than business and family, you are trying to add a new opposite-sex friend to the relationship, believe you, me. You got some 'splainin' to do, Lucy. Get your mind right before even broaching that conversation. Search your heart, and make sure it's worth it, and the same is true of social media friends.

Social Media "Friends"

From the words of Bobby Boucher's mama, Social media is the devil! Ok, maybe I'm being too harsh. It's not the devil, but it certainly leaves room to dance in the devil's playground, which is a detriment to any relationship. We all know the rules. You never invite trouble to your doorstep, and certainly not beyond. Still, despite cyberspace affording any one direct access into our homes and into our personal space, we engage. We engage knowing that with little effort, our spot can be blown up completely.

Social media makes possible and accessible desired sex friends by way of cyberspace. Because interaction is not in person, intimacy and flirtation often get swept under the rug as harmless banter. At least that's the cop out those who are guilty of these offenses will use to justify their actions. When in actuality, the same rules of engagement when dealing with opposite-sex friends should be applied and with even more care. That being said, one must proceed with extreme caution and tread lightly, keeping in mind the following.

Social media is all about appearance. So, if you appear to be guilty, you are guilty. Accordingly, inappropriate interaction on Facebook does not mean you are sending naked pictures or having cybersex. It does not have to be that extreme. Inappropriate interaction can take place in the implications of your actions rather than the acts themselves. People trolling by way of social media are looking for more than friendly conversation, and just responding to a person, in their minds, gives them hope, gives them leverage, and gives them opportunity. When in a committed relationship, the only person who should have any of these gratifications is your significant other. So, before engaging in social media antics, considering a few truths.

Male Perspective

Social media friends are not your friends. They are your companions. Therefore, they have no obligation, responsibility, or accountability to you or your mate. They have free reign to behave however they want with no concern for your wellbeing or the wellbeing of your relationship with said mate.

Social media is a permanent record of activity. Essentially, social media friends have done exactly what Smokey suggested Phylicia do in the movie *Friday*. They have remembered what was said, wrote it down, and took a picture for all to see. Understand that an incriminating record of accounts can always come back to bite you.

Social media gives people the courage to do things in the dark that they would not do in the light. Oh, but take heed. What's done in the dark is always brought to light. So...

1. Be Selective. Only respond to those with whom you need to respond.

2. Keep it Professional. When people DM you, and you do respond, lead with How may I help you? This sets the tone for a business transaction rather than a personal exchange.

3. React when necessary. People read a lot into likes and loves. Do not overuse either.

Be mindful the recipient is watching and may consider your comments an advance or window of opportunity for them to advance. Likewise, your mate is watching and is privy to the same information and, subsequently, the same feeling. Do not give him or her reason to feel threatened or unsure whether that window is indeed open.

4. Do Not Write Anything You Do Not Want Your Mate to See. They will see it.

5. Don't do for another what you are not doing for your mate. Whether posting pics or offering congratulatory praise, your

mate should not feel that any person is worth celebrating, in your eyes, more than they.

6. Never broadcast your personal disputes on social media. This opens all kinds of doors and windows and subjects both you and your mate to public scrutiny. This behavior is childish and has no place in a serious relationship.

7. 7. Love your mate out loud on social media. Don't live on social media as a single person while in a committed relationship. Leave no room for doubt. Make clear your loyalty.

Female Perspective

Much is lost in translation through social media. Your responsibility to your mate when choosing to pursue "friendships" that could be harmful to your relationship is to mitigate the risk of that harm occurring. So, while these steps may seem excessive, just know they help you CYA (cover your ass) and the A of your mate. It seems to me like a small price to pay in an effort to sustain the relationship you want to last. My advice is, play like Nike, and just do it!

Chapter 9: Surviving Hurt

Female Perspective

Hurt comes in several shapes, forms, and fashions, but unlike many of our welcomed guests, it's never late. In fact, it often shows up early and when you least expect it. It walks very softly and carries a big stick. It sneaks up on you without warning. It tends to linger and continues to make a significant impact long after it's gone. Consequently, we must be ready to deal with hurt at all times because we never know when it will rear its ugly head.

Usher released a song in the mid-2000s entitled "Let it Burn", and for years, this was a trusted motto when dealing with hurt. As I prepared to exit stage left from a role I no longer wanted to play, I would prepare myself mentally to "let it burn." I would delete numbers to mitigate contact if and when the fire got too hot. I would tell myself this too shall pass and like those Hebrew boys in the fiery furnace, I also will come out unscathed. However, what I learned as I progressed through life, is that while this strategy worked very well for my reasons and seasons, my lifetimes were a whole 'nother story.

Before I get too far ahead, let me explain what I mean by reasons, seasons, and lifetimes…

About ten years ago, I ran across a very powerful poem by an unknown author, and in this poem, I learned that people who come into your life are not always meant to stay. Some have entered your life for a specific reason, to complete a task perhaps, and others for a particular season. Maybe a particular skill set needed to be developed or honed from your dealings with this person BEFORE entering another chapter of your life. Whatever the case, these relationships are temporary and can be treated as such, which is why the burn method was a viable option.

The hurt would burn strong at the beginning of our dissolution but would shortly thereafter begin to subside. At the same time, that burn was diminishing, that reason or season would be making their exodus from my life. By the time the burn died out entirely, the offender would be out of my life completely. I would no longer be reminded of the hurt that particular person caused because out of sight typically resulted in out of mind. The incident was not rehashed repeatedly in future disputes, as there were no future disputes to have.

That chapter was closed and a part of my past, leaving me free to journey on. Conversely, those lifetimes hit differently.

With lifetimes, the flame doesn't get a chance to die out. How can it when you see your offender, aka significant other, regularly? Under these circumstances, the flame is continually receiving oxygen. While it may die down for a spell, it can easily pick up with the slightest gust of wind, and wind is to be expected, for with any relationship comes storms. For me, this, coupled with the fact that I'm a Scorpio and in my best Cardi voice...*If you beef with me, we beefing for evaaaaaaaaaa...* made the burn method useless. Therefore, I had to devise a different strategy for surviving hurt from a lifetime.

I feel compelled to note the word survive was used intentionally. The definition of survive is to continue to live or exist in spite of, which lifetimes, unlike reasons and seasons, do. Lifetimes remain alive in your life, and the hurt they give, right along with them. So, surviving is a realistic coping mechanism. To better illustrate, one might think of hurt from a lifetime like an incurable disease. You cannot get rid of it, but you can manage it and live a full life despite its presence. The key is knowing how.

Paramount to surviving any kind of hurt is having enough information about the offense to find a way to be ok. So, rather than turn off all the lights and hide from the pain when it comes knocking at your door like it's a Jehovah's Witness on Saturday morning, you have to meet it head-on.

You must talk through the hurt and hash things out. This step can be intimidating, scary even. Nonetheless, it's necessary and needs to take place as soon as you are in a space to receive whatever will be thrown at you, and preferably within days of the offense, not weeks or months. You never want a situation to fester so long it becomes a more significant issue than where it began. Nor should it go unaddressed so long that the ramifications have no effect on the other person.

Now, if the offense was so extreme that you have to do it later than sooner, then take the time you need and never conduct this transaction at the expense of your safety. If danger is a pre-eminent threat, you may want to demote that person to a reason or a season and keep it pushing. However, since we are talking about Black Love, I will assume we are past this point and ready to proceed with the hashing out.

The most critical part of the hashing out is the ability to engage in effective communication, a skill so many of us lack. The primary reason we lack in this area is because of our inability to listen. Many of us simply do not know how to listen. We were never really taught, but we gon' learn today!

I spent my entire professional career in sales listening for a living. While I excelled at every position requiring this skill set of me, I found it so much easier listening to my clients than listening to my lifetime, especially when I was hurt. So, what I had to do is start applying those best practices and strategies used in dealing with my clients when dealing with my lifetimes. My favorite concept on which to rely for listening is the LAIR process for its simplicity and effectiveness.

First, you are to **L**isten for understanding in lieu of listening to respond. This is extremely important because there is a huge difference. When a person listens to respond, he or she will only hear what is pertinent to them, and in doing so, will miss the message every single time. Your goal, at this juncture, is to expose the other's truth. So, clear your mind of any chatter. In other words, remove all bias and preconceived notions, and just be quiet. Remember, truth is relative and is riddled with perspective. So, you need to hear everything the other has to say regardless of where it might register on your Richter scale of importance, accuracy, and otherwise.

Second, you must **Ac**knowledge what the other person has said to you, keeping in mind the following. One does not have to agree to acknowledge what the other is feeling. If you cannot respond with an "I understand why you might feel that way," because you really don't; at least respond with an "I hear you." Vital to this process is both parties knowing they were heard. When this step is skipped, the rest feels like an interrogation, which puts people on the defensive. You will get nowhere when the other switches to defense mode. So, help them to give you what you're seeking, which is their God's honest truth, with as little contempt as possible.

The third step is to **In**quire. Ask open-ended questions of your mate, like help me understand, or tell me more. This allows for the person to answer without you having influenced their response. You may have heard the phrase leading the witness. Well, this is the opposite of that.

Lastly, for a deeper comprehension, **R**epeat what you understood, not what you heard. This is not a test of memory. This is a test of understanding. Use their words but in a way that makes sense to you to make sure you understood what was conveyed to you. If that person says that is not what they said, don't take offense. Simply repeat the inquiry step until you get it right and you both are on the same page.

Once you have a clear concise picture of what took place, you mitigate the risk of omissions and errors wreaking havoc in the future. You can deal with the offense head-on in its entirety and devise a real strategy on moving forward from this point and moving forward begins and ends with the same action — forgiveness. Forgiveness will make or break a union and is not a step we can overlook. It may take time, and a great deal of effort but must take place, regardless.

Male Perspective

Some disputes, like ones fueled by a difference of opinion, for example, will be easier to forgive than others. The issue could be just not knowing better and or not realizing what the other knows and values. The problem could be a failure to agree to disagree. The solution could be as simple as having a conversation and meeting of the minds, or a simple acknowledgment and respect for the other's perspective.

Boundary issues could be resolved by merely mapping out borderlines moving forward. Draw those lines in the sand, so the other knows not to cross or to tread lightly when doing so. We do that with city roads and streets, right? Solid lines mean do not cross at all. Dashed lines mean cross with caution. Those lines are there for a reason. If not, we would have chaos and a ton of accidents, which brings me to my next point.

Some offenses truly are accidents with no malicious intent. If you failed to map out those borderlines with your mate and for your mate throughout your relationship, as your need changed, you are as much at fault for the damages when crossed as they are, if not more. In my best Buddy Love voice, *I've seen no Thomas Guide to your ass on Amazon, so you must do the work of making the lines clear for your mates, yourselves.* With that being said, forgive them for they knew not what they did. Make clear the yellow and white lines. Continue your trek.

These disputes do not have to be a detriment and don't need to be any bigger than they are.

As a rule of thumb, ponder this. If the issue will not matter in five years, it should not matter in five minutes? So, treat it accordingly. Communicate often and in real-time as a solution to minor issues that will otherwise grow and take on a life of its own when unresolved. Unresolved issues lead to resentment, and resentment is to hurt what calcium is to bones. Don't let resentment fortify your hurt. Identify the hurt and face it head-on. Find the solution to the issue that works for both parties. Implement the solution and kill it before it multiplies. This way, instead of letting something trivial tear your relationship down, you are forgiving, correcting, and moving on, allowing that thing to build it up, instead. Consider these issues milestones and their resolutions, building blocks to elevate your relationship to higher heights.

Now, unfortunately, we know all hurts do not have simple solutions. Some are much more complex. That's life. So, important is knowing how to tackle the bigger hurts as well as we tackle the smaller. For example, infidelity is a big hurt to most and can in no way be reduced to a simple difference of opinion. Infidelity will most likely matter in five years. Infidelity breaks trust, one of the most critical components of love, and that is just not something that can be repaired overnight.

For some, only time and time apart can heal such a wound. Others may fare well with couples' therapy or individual counseling. Changes in behavior may be the solution, like eliminating alcohol from a diet, adjusting social hours, taking breaks from social media, and incorporating rules of engagement with the desired sex. Or, maybe the key to it all is spending more quality time together. The bottom line is that hurt has to be handled case by case. No blueprint exists except the one you and your mate create by way of trial and error. Whatever that thing is that makes it possible for you to forgive and to stay and survive that hurt, only you and God know, but being truthful with yourself and with each other is most important when seeking the road to forgiveness.

If your lifetime is all in and really working at healing a hurt... If he or she is accommodating all of your requests and changing their behaviors that put you two in this predicament, then you have to honor that effort. Be opened to forgive. Granted, this is no easy task at all. Nonetheless, if you decided that the love was bigger than the hurt, and you decided to stay, then you must allow the two of you to move past it. You cannot harp on it. You cannot continue to rehash it. You have to somehow let it go or start anew for both of your sakes. Forgiveness frees you to love again.

Another type of big hurt we must be mindful of is grief. We live in times where grief is commonplace. Gone are the days in which the process of natural selection is the preeminent looming danger. No, we have diseases tearing through our streets that have no respect of persons, age be damned. We, as black people, are facing the fight of our lives on all fronts. We are amid a global pandemic that has shaken everyone to their core. We are grieving the fact we cannot show love like we used to through fellowship and congregation. Businesses are shutting down left and right. People are out of work with no idea of how they will survive. People of all ages, of all races, of all nations, are dying at the hand of this disease that steals their breath.

In addition, I am sad to report that in 2021 civil unrest is at the height it was in the 60s. We have a civil war on our home front as blacks continue to fight the same fight for our lives that we've fought since the end of "plantation" slavery. Our people are being massacred by those who swore to protect us. And… Let us not fail to mention the tribal war ripping our community to shreds as many of us fall victim to the self-hate, the systemic racism and the institutionalized racism designed for us to commit genocide.

We are living in the most tumultuous times America has seen in over a century. Grief, for Black Love, is the big hurt boogie man right now. He is under every bed lurking at every corner. How does one survive? Strike that. How do two survive a big hurt like grief?

First and foremost, understand what you are dealing with. Grief is a big hurt that causes immense pain, and immense pain manifests itself in many ways. It looks like sickness. It expresses itself by way of anger and depression. It attempts to curtail itself by way of self-medication. It is often uncontained and uncontrollable and lashes out at will. Pain is a force to be reckoned with not just for the inflicted but also for the caretaker of the inflicted. Pain makes loving a person hard, but that's exactly what we are charged with doing. We must love one another past the pain.

The Bible talks about fruits of the spirit and no better way to give yourself a fighting chance at your relationship surviving this type of hurt than to implement your fruits. The fruits of the spirit are love, joy, peace, patience, kindness, goodness, faithfulness, gentleness, and self-control.

Show love by being selfless and making the other's needs a priority. Allow for times that aren't always about you. Show joy engaging in dialogue and activity that makes your mate smile. Bring peace by creating a warm, safe, stress-free environment in which one can recuperate. Exercise patience, allowing the other grace and mercy. Understand that everyone's reaction to grief will be different and has little to do with you. Don't take personally what manifests from grief when you were not the cause.

Demonstrate kindness with affection and reassurance. Be good to the person and do right. Make no attempt to exploit their vulnerability. Be faithful in your well-doing and with the care you provide your mate. Do not give up on them. Critical to their recovery is knowing they can count on someone and not have to get through the pain alone.

Be gentle and protective of the other's heart, minding your mannerisms and bridling your tongue. Exercise self-control. Refrain from any action or reaction that can make the situation worse.

Remember the Bible instructs in all things great and small, to lean not unto our own understanding. In all ways acknowledge God, and He will direct our path. He is the only provider of peace that passes all understanding, and that comes in pretty handy when surviving hurt. Don't hesitate to try Him.

Lastly, for all involved, do not bring past hurt as baggage into a current situation. Trust and believe your current situation will render enough baggage of its own to carry on this journey. Your mate cannot carry, cannot repent for, cannot cure, and cannot resolve something he or she is not guilty of and took no part in. Don't expect them to. Heed the airport's warning. When you see baggage that does not belong to you, leave it! Do not pick it up. Do not approach it. Seek out a professional who will find the right way to dispose of it or return it to its rightful place. If, through these processes of discovery, you find you have baggage from previous relationships, seek the professional help you need for disposal and or return to its rightful place. Continue, carrying nothing but the baggage for you and your mate's current journey.

Chapter 10: Make It Last Forever

I don't know about you, but I find fascinating the wisdom in the lyrics of some of the most simplistic songs. Take Keith Sweat's "Make it Last Forever" released over thirty years ago. When Keith Sweat first crooned the lyrics to his hit song, I was so caught up in the tune's catchiness and matching Jacci McGhee note for note that I failed to realize the value in its content. Now, I know better.

One of the things that makes this song so compelling for me is the realization that "Make it Last Forever, a timeless love song, is a song consisting mostly of demands. Even the hook was a highly emphasized string of commands.

"Oh… OO…Make it last forever. Don't let our love end!"

This classic, played at more than 90% of all black weddings, is little more than a series of orders, orders that the receiving party could either adhere to or defy. So, what does that tell us?

The lyrics to "Make It Last Forever" tell us that doing so is not an occurrence. It is a choice. It is not a whim. It is a decision. It is not reactive. It is proactive. Making it last forever only happens where intent and purpose drive activity.

For example, telling your mate what you want and need from them, as encouraged in the first chapter of this book, is an intentional and purpose-driven action designed to achieve the desired result that can propel you and your mate closer to forever. Keith demonstrates this action at the start of his song, cosigning an undeniable truth. Telling is the only action that creates a sustainable love culture, one in which essential information flows freely between two people in a relationship, making possible a united stand against time.

Now, I do understand the ideology that your mate is supposed to be able to anticipate your needs, but that also takes time; and what we must also consider is that our needs change, and they do so frequently. Ergo, all the time in the world won't nullify telling as a cultural necessity in cultivating a sustainable love. As previously instructed, tell him what you want, and tell her what you need. Don't be timid about it. Then and only then are you giving your relationship a real chance at forever.

Another point of context I deem most powerful about this song and congruent with the words in this manual is the fact it is a call and response. More specifically, it is a call to action and response with action. "Make it Last Forever" tells us to meet love with love. Simply put, react to your mate's call with the desired action. When able, give them what they want. It's ok to do so. If your mate is willing to be vulnerable with you, be gracious, and yes, in some cases, vulnerable in return. Don't ignore his or her plea. Take heed, unless, of course, you really don't want to make it last forever.

The wise and prophetic Miss Erykah Badu clearly concurred with Keith when she predicted, *"I betcha love will make it better."* I'm betting the same. I bet you can rest assured that love will make it better. When has it not? It is the first commandment with promise. Therefore, make a point to love hard, love loud, and love long. Make love a priority. Don't keep it a mystery. Don't put it on lock. Don't take it away. Don't be stingy with love. Let it be known by way of your words and your actions that you are committed wholeheartedly to making it last forever with your mate. When your mate asks you to tell them you love them, need them and want them, respond accordingly…

Let me tell you how much I love you

Let me tell you that I really need you…
No one but you, baby
Can make me feel
The way you make me, make me, make me feel…

… and watch what happens. Watch you and your mate fall in love over and over again.

Now, something else I took note of. When listening carefully to the words of the song, considering the structure and back-and-forth banter, this struck me as familiar. Does this lyrical waltz not resemble Solomon and his Shulamite bride? Solomon offered his bride this same type of assurance at the onset of their relationship because assurance was necessary for her to feel comfortable enough to embark upon forever, hence its rightful place and importance in the trek to forever. However, embark means to begin, and forever is not just a beginning. Forever extends beyond the beginning and accordingly, warrants something that does not expire the moment it takes place.

So what comes next?

Reassurance! Reassurance is the evolution of assurance. It is that variation of assurance that is recurring and takes place, the morning after and the morning after that, and the morning after that…

Reassurance is that intentional, purposeful act that serves as motivation for your mate to cling to your side beyond the beginning and well into forever. Continue to dote on one another, making clear the passion and desire and love you have for each other until you reach forever.

>*…Ooh, give me kisses (Kisses)*
>*Love me (Love me), hold me (Hold me)*
>*Squeeze me (Squeeze me)*
>*Chillin' (Chillin'), come on (Come on)*
>*I love you (You know I do), baby*

Complete these aforementioned tasks daily, for these are the tasks that reassure your mate that he or she is all you want and need. Do so without ceasing, so there is no doubt. Continue with consistency, to do that work that keeps your mate engaged… the work that seduces the mental, puts them at ease and takes away all the pains of the day… the work that makes toes curl and bodies quiver… the work that makes a person long for forever.

The blueprint to a successful, enduring, forever love is to keep loving, and so it seems, the question and the answer are one and the same: How do we make it last forever? We make it last forever by making it last forever!

Author Bio: Bobbie Michelle Bean

Bobbie Michelle Bean is a mother, real estate agent, investor, entrepreneur, public speaker, and author. Bobbie writes fiction based on real-life, reconstructed biographies, and allegories from which to obtain wisdom and understanding meant to aid the journey through life.

Bobbie's in-depth understanding of human action revealed in her debut novel, *Through Blind Eyes*, is further authenticated in her latest endeavor, *Essence of Black Love: The Blueprint,* as she explores the intricacies of black love through history, culture, music, and the Word, and offers instruction and applications to fortify black love and forge bonds that last forever.

Bobbie received her bachelor's degree from the University of Cincinnati and her master's degree from South University, where her concentrations of study at both were behavioral sciences. Her studies, in conjunction with a long, successful career in sales as well as her own personal life lessons, make her extremely knowledgeable about human behavior, human emotion, and forced or triggered emotional response.

When not writing, mothering, entrepreneuring, or public speaking, renaissance woman and Cincinnati native Bobbie Michelle Bean can be found working desperately to shed her stomach in time for her late summer wedding; sadly, to no avail. Her favorite day of the week is still mommy/ daughter day with her now-adult nineteen-year-old daughter. She dances in the rain, sings in the shower, cooks big dinners for her family, and emulates black love in every way possible.

Dedication

This book is dedicated to my morning sun, my cup of tea, my shining star, the best of me, my amazing and beautiful daughter, Myshon Hudgies. You are my motivation.

To my parents Bobby and Mary Bean, thank you. You have shown me for forty-eight years, the fortitude of black love. I cannot express in words what it means to see you in your golden years, all day laughing and loving and enjoying one another. It's a blessing to my soul. Because of you, I know Who God is, and I truly understand what love is.

To fiancé, Steven Alexander, the superhero to whom I am his rib. I love you dearly. Thank you for supporting me in all my endeavors, loving me through all my crazy, and standing with me against all odds. I cannot wait to see forever with you.

-Bobbie Michelle Bean

Author Bio: Donny Young

Donny Young is a Cincinnati native and a huge Bengals fan (Who Dey!). He is a serial entrepreneur who owns a promotion company, a clothing line, a security company, and is heavily vested in real estate, but it does not stop there. Donny Young now has the honor of adding to his list of professional accomplishments, Co-author of *Essence of Black Love: The Blueprint*.

Of all Donny's impressive accomplishments and accolades, most important in his life is his beautiful wife that he has been married to for nearly ten years, and three wonderful children, ages twenty-one, fifteen, and six.

As you can imagine, with all Mr. Young is juggling, family life can get a little hectic, but Donny takes it all in stride, cherishing each moment with his wife and children in whom he finds such gratification. Donny states, "I am so proud and take so much pride in my family. Family is my foundation."

Well, we can all be thankful it is, for it is that foundation that inspired Donny to co-author a masterpiece in *Essence of Black Love: The Blueprint*, a piece of literature we all can learn and grow from.

Dedication

This book is dedicated to my beautiful wife Ebony Young, who shows me every day the true meaning of black love.

To my beautiful mother, Hilda Young, and grandmother Leureen Hicks, I would not know a love like this had it not been for the two of you. You both showed me how to love and appreciate and care for a black woman, and I know you are proud of the legacy she and I have created. I feel the two of you watching over us every day and love you both dearly.

To my aunts Linda Hicks and Joyce Williamson, who are here to witness the legacy and to be my village, thank you. To my Uncle Charles Hicks, thank you for demonstrating by action more than words what it means to be a man with strong principles and a great work ethic. I pray I have made every one of you proud.

Lastly, to my children, Taylor, Donovan, and Hillary Young, thank you for making me a better man. Every day I watch you grow is a day I cherish forever.

-Donny Young

Made in the USA
Monee, IL
19 February 2021

60903050R00069